ACKNOWLEDGEMENTS

Many people contributed to the creation of this guidance, from conceptualization and planning through implementation, and finally to the publication before you. Throughout this project, the National Planning team contributed their time and expertise on policing strategies, civil rights and civil liberties protections, and immigrant and minority community perspectives. Their expertise and guidance helped launch this project and ensure the dialogs were productive, which was invaluable in shaping this initiative.

We are very grateful to each of the pilot sites who willingly hosted roundtables in their jurisdictions:

❖ Boston Police Department

❖ Miami-Dade Police Department

❖ Seattle Police Department

❖ Texas Department of Public Safety

The lessons learned and information gathered at these sessions is directly reflected in these pages, and this document could not have been produced without their support and participation.

This guidance would not have been possible without the community partners who attended the roundtables, ready to work together to build trust, sharing freely their concerns and perspectives, and bringing with them the many excellent recommendations that are echoed in this report. The diversity of those partners is illustrative of the great strength of our communities.

We are also grateful for the people who worked so diligently behind the scenes to provide the recommendations within this report:

Susan B. Reingold, Office of the Program Manager, Information Sharing Environment; **Thomas J. O'Reilly,** U.S. Department of Justice, Bureau of Justice Assistance; **John Cohen,** U.S. Department of Homeland Security; **Amy Schapiro,** U.S. Department of Justice, Office of Community Oriented Policing Services; **Katherine G. Black,** Office of the Program Manager, Information Sharing Environment; **Elizabeth Neumann,** Office of the Program Manager, Information Sharing Environment for their vision, leadership, and tireless participation as this very important initiative evolved.

Robert Wasserman, for capturing the many ideas and recommendations from each of the roundtables, and putting pen to paper to create this guidance.

Bob Cummings, Angel Ganey, Terri Pate, and **Diane Ragans** for their invaluable logistic support.

Lastly, we are grateful for the funding and programmatic support from the Office of the Program Manager, Information Sharing Environment (PM-ISE), and support from the U.S Department of Justice, Bureau of Justice Assistance, U.S. Department of Justice Office of Community Oriented Policing Services, and the U.S. Department of Homeland Security.

EXECUTIVE SUMMARY

The Building Communities of Trust (BCOT) initiative focuses on developing relationships of trust between law enforcement, fusion centers, and the communities they serve, particularly immigrant and minority communities, so that the challenges of crime control and prevention of terrorism can be addressed. Lessons learned have been documented from a series of roundtable discussions held across the country in the past year between state and major urban area fusion centers, local law enforcement, and community advocates. The resulting BCOT Guidance provides advice and recommendations on how to initiate and sustain trusting relationships that support meaningful sharing of information, responsiveness to community concerns and priorities, and the reporting of suspicious activities that appropriately distinguish between innocent cultural behaviors and behavior that may legitimately reflect criminal enterprise or terrorism precursor activities.

The evolving nature of immigrant and minority communities, and the importance for communities and law enforcement to build and maintain trusting relationships to prevent acts of crime and terrorism, is the overarching theme of this Guidance. Within this context, community policing is described as a successful strategy that can be used by law enforcement to collaborate and partner with local communities, particularly immigrant and minority populations.

The Guidance describes the challenges that must be addressed by fusion centers, local law enforcement agencies, and communities in developing these relationships of trust. These challenges can only be met if privacy, civil rights and civil liberties are protected. For fusion centers, this requires strong privacy policies and audits of center activities to ensure that the policies and their related standards are being fully met. For law enforcement agencies, it means that meaningful dialog and collaboration with communities needs to occur in a manner that increases legitimacy of the agency in the eyes of that community. Law enforcement must establish legitimacy in the communities they serve if trusting relationships are to be established. For communities, their leaders and representatives must collaborate with law enforcement and share responsibility for addressing the problems of crime and terrorism prevention in their neighborhoods.

Recommendations

The recommendations set forth in the Guidance fall into three areas: fusion centers, law enforcement, and communities.

Fusion Centers

❖ Increase cultural sensitivity of analysts so they understand the difference between behavior that is indicative of criminal or terrorist activity and that which is constitutionally protected to prevent improper or inaccurate assumptions.

❖ Ensure transparency, form an advisory board comprised of nonlaw enforcement members, and make it part of the decision-making process.

❖ Provide meaningful and independent oversight of intelligence processes, ensuring that privacy, civil rights, and civil liberties are protected in accordance with the law and fusion center privacy policies.

❖ Ensure that fusion center products and activities are useful to law enforcement in their efforts to address crime and prevent terrorism.

❖ Work to make the fusion center useful to local communities, beyond law enforcement.

Law Enforcement

❖ Train front-line officers on the suspicious activity reporting (SAR) process so officers understand their role and how the information is used.

❖ Define and develop an understanding among police officers about how trusting relationships are beneficial to them to reduce crime and prevent terrorism.

❖ Ensure that diversity is institutionalized throughout the fabric of policing, providing the law enforcement agency and its employees with information on diverse cultures and improved access to minority and immigrant communities.

❖ Move law enforcement agencies beyond just community relations so that all officers understand how to engage with immigrant and minority communities and can thus provide a felt and positive presence in these neighborhoods.

❖ Answer community questions about SAR and intelligence process in a manner that ensures transparency.

❖ Address community concerns that arise from transparency by collaborating with the community on policy development and related actions.

❖ Embrace the community policing philosophy by emphasizing partnerships and problem solving.

Community

❖ Recognize the importance of information sharing to help prevent crime and terrorism in their neighborhoods; meet with community leadership in both private and open forums to accelerate information sharing and ensure discussion concerning possible threats to their communities.

❖ Become part of the problem-solving process through community policing, thus having the community share responsibility for addressing the problems of crime and terrorism prevention.

❖ Involve community representatives in cultural awareness training for new recruits, with the training occurring in the community, not at the academy.

INTRODUCTION

The Building Communities of Trust (BCOT) initiative focuses on developing relationships of trust between law enforcement, state and major urban area fusion centers, and the communities they serve, particularly immigrant and minority communities, to address the challenges of crime control and prevention of terrorism. Being effective in these areas requires meaningful sharing of information and collaboration among law enforcement agencies, and between the community and police.

The role of the community, together with law enforcement and fusion centers, is crucially important to safeguarding our society from real threats posed by violent extremists. First Amendment protected freedoms such as religion, speech, and assembly should not and cannot be used as the sole grounds for launching investigative actions. Such actions undermine effective community-based counter-radicalization efforts and may even be viewed as an invitation by violent extremists to target society further. Enough damage has already been done to minority communities who have been unfairly branded by the rhetoric or actions of a tiny minority of violent extremists.

BCOT specifically seeks to explore the intersection of three critical partners—the community, local law enforcement, and fusion centers—in our nation's framework to improve information sharing and collaboration in order to protect our local communities. The knowledge about communities that comes from trust-based relationships among such partners is critical because it allows law enforcement officers and analysts to distinguish between innocent cultural behavior and that indicative of criminal activity.

As federal, state, local, and tribal governments have worked to improve the sharing of terrorism-related information, a concurrent top priority has been to ensure the protection of information privacy rights, civil rights, and civil liberties of Americans. The BCOT initiative represents a critical next step toward ensuring that the concerns of privacy, civil rights and civil liberties advocates, and community groups are addressed as the capabilities of law enforcement agencies to gather information, analyze, store, and share critical information improve and are formalized. Up to this point, the dialog between law enforcement and community stakeholders has happened primarily at the national level. However, information sharing processes and technologies are also implemented locally. As a result, we must also engage in a dialog at the local level, involving people who live and work in the very communities we seek to protect from crime and violence, and addressing those activities that may be related to international and domestic terrorism.

Trust, transparency, and the protection of privacy, civil rights, and civil liberties are fundamental to effective crime control, and these principles must serve as the foundation for information and intelligence sharing efforts intended to support crime and terrorism prevention activities. Through a series of facilitated sessions, the BCOT effort convened privacy, civil rights and civil liberties groups, community leaders, and law enforcement officials for an intensive dialog. The program's objective is to bring about a better understanding by communities of how law enforcement is using information to protect neighborhoods and citizens, while at the same time educating law enforcement on the priorities and needs of residents and how various community members view law enforcement efforts. Forging trusting relationships between local officials and community members serves as the foundation for improved communication.

Focus of Trusting Relationships

The BCOT pilot specifically focused on the development of trusting relationships that support the Information Sharing Environment in the areas of state and major urban area fusion centers, the Nationwide Suspicious Activity Reporting Initiative (NSI), and community policing.

FUSION CENTERS. Owned and operated by state and local governments, fusion centers are an important analytic and information sharing resource that supports the efforts of state and local officials to prevent and investigate crime in their communities and address our most pressing national challenges—such as gangs, border violence, narcotics, homicides, natural disasters, and terrorism.

NSI. The NSI is an effort to establish a standardized nationwide capacity for gathering, documenting, processing, analyzing, storing, and sharing terrorism-related suspicious activity reports (Information Sharing Environment SARs—ISE SARs) in a manner that rigorously protects the privacy, civil rights, and civil liberties of Americans.[1] An ISE SAR is official documentation of observed behavior reasonably indicative of preoperational planning related to terrorism or other criminal activity. The NSI process is a cycle of 12 interrelated operational activities that are grouped under five standardized business process activities: planning; gathering and processing; analysis and production; dissemination; and reevaluation. The effort is an outgrowth of a number of separate but related activities during the past several years, as called for in the 2007 National Strategy for Information Sharing.

The Federal Government believes that achieving a national network of state and major urban area fusion centers is important to national security and is utilizing these centers as primary focal points within the state and local environment for the receipt and sharing of terrorism-related information. The fusion centers, operating locally, customize such information to address intra- or interstate needs. Fusion centers exist to provide critical state and local information and subject-matter expertise to officials at all levels, including the communication of locally generated terrorism-related information back to the Federal Government—all in a manner that, like the NSI, is designed to rigorously protect the privacy, civil rights, and civil liberties of Americans.

---

1   Further information on the NSI can be found at http://nsi.ncirc.gov/default.aspx

COMMUNITY POLICING. In the last 20 years, community policing has been acknowledged as the most effective policing strategy for addressing crime, building stronger crime-resistant communities, and increasing resident satisfaction with the quality of policing services in their neighborhoods. Across the country, there have been numerous examples of successful law enforcement and community collaborations toward crime prevention and neighborhood problem solving. Yet, some law enforcement agencies have faced challenges when learning how to establish collaborative, meaningful relationships with the communities they serve. While there are numerous examples of success, the lessons learned have not been universally adopted. The Police Executive Research Forum noted that effective community policing demands law enforcement's awareness of community concerns, sensitivity to cultural norms and practices, and an open dialog about policing tactics that will help law enforcement eliminate fear and enhance protection in diverse communities.[2]

The Challenge of Developing Trusting Relationships

The need for law enforcement officers to engage their communities to prevent crime and terrorism is an ongoing priority among law enforcement agencies. In particular, this engagement is critical for law enforcement officers to be able to put potentially suspicious activity into context with the cultural norms of their community.

The NSI provides a standardized approach, including training, to ensure the legal gathering, documenting, and processing of SARs (observed behavior reasonably indicative of preoperational planning related to terrorism or other criminal activity). It affirms that reported behaviors are sufficiently vetted to identify and share only those SARs that have a potential terrorism nexus (are reasonably indicative of criminal activity associated with terrorism). The NSI further ensures that appropriate terrorism-related SARs are transmitted to the

---

2   Heather J. Davies et al., *Protecting Your Community from Terrorism: Strategies for Local Law Enforcement, Volume 2: Working With Diverse Communities.* Washington, D.C. Police Executive Research Forum, 2004, p. 2.

FBI's Joint Terrorism Task Force (JTTF). There are many sources of suspicious activity reporting, including the community itself, law enforcement, public agencies, and private sector entities. Any reported information must always be considered in the context of the cultural norms of the relevant community. For example, for several years now, police officers have been responding to observations of citizens concerned about "suspicious persons" who may be in the community conducting surveillance of potential victims or other targets of opportunity. The challenge for both law enforcement and the community is to make sure that reported suspicion is not based upon inherent prejudice or bias, thus making it more essential for law enforcement to understand the communities they serve.

Although there have been pockets of success in building trusting relationships with diverse communities, challenges remain. Lack of trust is one of the greatest obstacles faced by American policing and has a direct impact on the ability to address neighborhood issues of crime, disorder, and the prevention of terrorism.

Law enforcement officers, like many others in our society, are often unsure how best to initiate dialog with persons and groups who they are not familiar with. Although law enforcement managers are often better at reaching out to their diverse communities to establish relationships, many executives recognize the challenge for their officers in developing effective relationships at the neighborhood level.

It is imperative that fusion centers understand the communities they serve in order to produce analysis that is valuable to local law enforcement while protecting the privacy, civil rights, and civil liberties of Americans. Fusion center personnel must also be sure to not inadvertently generate reports based on stereotypes, assumptions, or erroneous information, particularly since such products can cause damage to any relationship with the community.

Privacy, civil rights, and civil liberties advocates as well as news media have highlighted inappropriate content in a few fusion centers' products, which has caused concern about the role and function of fusion centers and perpetuated a general misunderstanding of their mission. These fusion center products made generalizations that were inaccurate, out of context, or insensitive, furthering distrust. Privacy, civil rights, and civil liberties training for fusion center analysts has been instituted to prevent such mistakes in the future.

The findings of the *IACP 2007 National Summit on Intelligence: Gathering, Sharing, Analysis, and Use after 9-11*[3] concluded that local law enforcement often has a limited understanding of the purpose and nature of fusion centers and how they can be beneficial in supporting the Information Sharing Environment. The summit noted: "Beyond adopting an all-crimes approach to information sharing, fusion center directors and law enforcement executives ought to reaffirm their commitment to working together to improve the utility of centers."[4]

In reality, fusion centers are inextricably tied to both local law enforcement and their communities. If local law enforcement and their communities develop mutual trust, they will be able to work together to identify suspicious activities that may indicate criminal activity, some of which may have a direct terrorism nexus. Putting information into the appropriate context is essential to the fusion center's development of accurate analytic products that are free from bias and reflect where our communities or the nation may be at risk—particularly in the areas of radicalization and violent extremist behaviors. Through these relationships, local law enforcement, operating under community policing principles, can provide fusion centers with an understanding of the cultural context in which they must process the information that they receive.

Developing trust is complex. It requires an open mind, a willingness to listen and consider another person's perspective, an understanding of the person's culture and environment, and a commitment to honesty in the relationship.

---

3   The IACP 2007 National Summit on Intelligence: Gathering, Sharing, Analysis, and Use after 9-11 was held on November 27–28, 2007 with support from the U.S. Department of Justice Office of Community Oriented Policing Services; the U.S. Department of Homeland Security; and the Office of the Program Manager for the Information Sharing Environment.
4   National Summit, op. cit., p. 21.

For a law enforcement agency, it becomes important to respect diversity and to celebrate the potential for bringing people with different cultures and lifestyles together into the basic fabric of a strong diverse community environment. In some cities, law enforcement agencies have been at the forefront of creating that environment. It is important that fusion centers be sensitive to the cultural norms of diverse communities as they frame their products and reports, and as they interact with the community.

For law enforcement and fusion centers to develop relationships of trust, it is crucial that they recognize that racial, religious, ethnic, and other minority communities all have an interest in addressing behaviors that negatively impact the stability of the community. It has been common practice for law enforcement officers and fusion center analysts to primarily focus on perceived offenders, and not prioritize the importance of having strong trusting relationships with the community. It is leaders or residents of neighborhoods who are often best positioned to know who in the community may be at risk of criminal activity, whether it is dealing drugs or terrorism activities. When youth begin to adopt a life of criminal activity, whether it is joining a terrorist organization or a local gang, it rarely occurs without someone from that community noticing a change in behavior.

From the community's perspective, respect must be earned. Communities that do not trust law enforcement are often unwilling to share their observations and knowledge unless they feel the officers are committed to fair and equal treatment of community members. Without strong partnerships, a perception can develop that law enforcement is the enemy. Without mutual trust, the community may not have the benefit of all relevant information about potential threats, and therefore not share information about suspicious activity that may be a risk to the safety of the community. Constructively engaging the community to address the problems of crime and disorder that threaten quality of life relies on the development of relationships that are based on understanding divergent cultures, respecting individuals and their perspectives, and listening to community priorities and norms.

During various times in American history, law enforcement has had strained relationships with various communities and interests. While the fabric of society continues to change, current events are likely to continue to place a certain strain between law enforcement and the public. For example, the 9/11 attacks sparked tension between law enforcement and minority populations that felt they were under scrutiny because of their religious or ethnic backgrounds. For example, immigrant populations may have a fear of law enforcement resulting from their own negative experiences and persecution in their homelands. By that same measure, law enforcement executives understand that their officers are not always familiar with the vast number of cultures and languages they encounter while protecting and serving their communities.

Many law enforcement agencies have made considerable strides toward hiring a more diverse work force and incorporating community policing into their daily practices. In communities across this country, large and small, law enforcement has acted as a convener to help bridge the gap between immigrant populations and the police. These efforts have led to the fostering of environments of trust through community outreach. While still in their infancy, fusion centers can learn from law enforcement's positive experiences in working with the community and the importance of framing discussions in a manner that respects and is sensitive to how these communities view their world.

In addressing neighborhood crime, police must demonstrate that they care about the neighborhood and its problems. Likewise, fusion centers should partner with local law enforcement in these endeavors. By taking proactive steps to develop trust and transparency within the communities they serve, both local police and the fusion center can help to build community awareness of a local fusion center and its purpose, policies, and operating methods—and gain a better understanding of the local environment. There should also be a feedback mechanism developed that allows community members to express relevant concerns in a positive, educational, and reasoned manner when actions by local law enforcement or the fusion center result in mistakes or are done in a manner that erodes trust. The fusion center should have a redress policy or procedure in place to address concerns.

The Evolving Nature of Immigrant and Minority Communities

In recent years, new groups have come to the United States and have formed new minority and immigrant communities. Logically, new immigrants have moved to areas in which others from similar backgrounds have settled. These growing communities bring with them new customs, traditions, and ways of life that are often unfamiliar to others living around them. As a result, discrimination or inappropriate behavior may arise from misunderstanding or previous negative relationships. Compounding this challenge is the fact that members of these new immigrant communities also may not fully understand how this country's laws and criminal justice processes work.

Since some terrorists have been identified as members of specific immigrant or minority groups, suspicion of all members of these groups has tended to grow, encompassing those who have no involvement in terrorist or criminal activity. This has the added problem of making it difficult for law enforcement and the government to establish relationships of trust, or even to effectively and constructively engage these communities to better understand their concerns and issues—particularly with relation to criminal activity or potential terrorism.

The Importance of Trust in Crime and Terrorism Prevention

There are strong links between crime and terrorism, as those who intend to carry out terrorist acts often engage in criminal enterprises to fund their activities. Terrorist acts and crime events can have a devastating impact on community life. Patterns of crime are no longer limited to a single geographic area, city, or neighborhood, and while predictive policing methods attempt to identify patterns of criminality and prevent the next crime from occurring, the willingness to share information is critical to this process.

In many areas, communities are unwilling to share information with the police because they do not know what will happen to the information. Law enforcement agencies can be unwilling to share information with other agencies because they want to keep control of what enforcement actions are taken. And both community and police may sometimes be reluctant to share information with federal law enforcement agencies because they perceive that those agencies were unwilling to share information with them.

The BCOT Methodology

Roundtable discussions were organized in four different locations around the country (three localities and one state) with a diverse group of representatives from the local community, law enforcement, and fusion center leadership to explore how to effectively engage in meaningful and ongoing dialog. Lessons learned from these discussions have been used to develop this Guidance. The primary focus was engaging minority and immigrant communities; specifically those residents of neighborhoods with diverse cultures that often do not have strong collaborative relationships with the police.

This project was designed to:

❖ Gather representative views of community leaders regarding strategies for developing and sustaining trust

❖ Gather representative views of police executives about the type of training and guidance that will be most useful to police executives and their employees

❖ Gather vignettes about successful "best practices" as models for adoption

❖ Identify best practices that assist fusion center analysts to better understand their local communities and cultures

❖ Develop guidance for fusion centers, emphasizing the importance of outreach and transparency, and working with local police in developing sensitivity to local community issues

❖ Develop guidance for law enforcement agencies regarding the importance of collaborating with fusion centers to understand minority and immigrant community issues that need to be addressed in developing relationships of trust.

Current Efforts to Improve Interaction

There are numerous creative ways to support the development of trusting relationships; some of the more successful strategies involve:

❖ Community outreach through community policing

❖ New models of training for officers

❖ Community forums

❖ Establish Terrorism Liaison Officers/Fusion Liaison Officers/Crime Prevention Officers

❖ Increased diversity within the police department at all levels

❖ Development of community background materials.

A strong executive commitment to community policing is important to developing the needed base for future actions, with training being a strategy that can assist in this effort. Officers must know how to initiate conversations with those who don't have trust in police, based on past experiences. Many officers find it difficult to interact with neighborhood residents and develop a "felt presence" in congested, urban neighborhoods populated with different cultures that they may not understand. Producing background materials on different cultures, as was done in the Ohio Fusion Center, demonstrates how institutions can have a major impact in educating personnel. It also illustrates to the ethnic and minority communities that cultural understanding is a priority. Additionally, as the Massachusetts Bay Transit Authority have learned, using good models for training police on police-youth interaction can dramatically change such relationships.

In the United Kingdom, British police have instituted a new level of police officer called "community support officer;" paraprofessionals who develop neighborhood relationships, facilitate discussions, and provide response to neighborhood problems often difficult for patrol officers to have time to address. These diverse groups of officers have developed trusting relationships with community leaders in a manner that has dramatically increased the communication between neighborhood leaders and the police.

Ensuring that the police force is diverse is an important underpinning of all these efforts. The recruitment of minority officers—particularly from immigrant communities—can be challenging, but the development of trusting relationships can go a long way toward meeting this goal.

Community forums, such as those held by this project, can lay important foundations for future discussions on issues of concern to communities, showing a commitment to listening to localized concerns, and energetic follow-up after the meeting.

The following are a series of specific recommendations based on feedback from the BCOT pilot discussions.

RECOMMENDATIONS FOR FUSION CENTERS

Fusion centers can greatly improve their impact by identifying and establishing meaningful relationships with significant partners at the state and local levels, and ensuring transparency by explaining their purpose to the community.

Increasing Cultural Awareness Among Analysts

It is important that analysts understand the importance of bias-free reporting. Inappropriate use of race, religion, gender, and other related factors to form judgments is unacceptable but also greatly harms the credibility of fusion centers and creates a widespread perception of bias and mistrust, which can take years to restore. Analysis must be based on behaviors rather than other factors that may be interpreted as bias. The behaviors identified as part of the NSI are a good place to base behavioral analysis, since they have been documented against a 10-year database of precursor activities that have preceded terrorism events in the United States and around the world. A potential resource for analysts is the DOJ Office of Justice Programs, Privacy and Civil Liberties, Training Resources for State, Local and Tribal Fusion Centers, which provides resources and training materials.[5]

❖ **The role of local police.** Because fusion centers often have limited interaction with area communities, they may have to rely on community-based information. In the best circumstances, local police will have substantial relationships of trust with members of those communities. Absent that, the fusion center will have to work through the local police agency to establish those relationships.

---

5   More information on the DOJ Office of Justice Programs, Privacy and Civil Liberties, Training Resources for State, Local and Tribal Fusion Centers may be found at www.it.ojp.gov/default.aspx?area=privacy&page=1258

Establishing a strong liaison officer program is an effective means of engaging with local agencies on these relationships. The joint DHS/DOJ Fusion Process Technical Assistance Program has numerous materials available on establishing a strong liaison officer program.[6]

Fusion center personnel understand how threats apply to local communities and provide analysis that can help front-line officers put behavior into context. This includes behaviors that are associated with criminal activity or are specifically not associated with such activity but are a part of the cultural tradition of local immigrant and minority communities. Local police, in turn, can provide important input to fusion centers in understanding these differences.

❖ **The impact of cultural misunderstanding, misinterpretation and miscommunication.** An issue of great importance for fusion centers, as it is for local police, is to understand the cultural norms of a particular community so that normal cultural behaviors are not mistaken for potentially suspicious activity. This knowledge and understanding requires substantial interaction with these communities, something local police are best positioned to undertake. When cultural norms are not understood, analytical products may reflect assumptions about suspicious activity that are not only inaccurate but insensitive to the communities involved, potentially leading to an increase in mistrust of policing efforts.

❖ **Establishing cultural competency.** There are a number of ways in which cultural sensitivity can be achieved. Experience has shown the best way to do this is by engaging in dialog on issues of concern to the community and the police. As described later in this guidance, this requires careful listening, engaging in discussions, respect for different cultures, and interest in knowing more about a particular group and its history. There are many diversity training courses that focus on these issues, and they can provide a helpful foundation; however, few courses are as effective as in-person interaction and discussion.

---

6   See Establishing a Fusion Liaison Officer Program. Washington, D.C: Department of Justice/Department of Homeland Security, October 2009.

❖ **Cultural sensitivity and acceptable terminology.** When dealing with topics such as race, religion, and culture, it is important to understand the cultural norms and behaviors of diverse populations. Without this awareness, there is the potential for statements to be made that will unintentionally offend a person or group. Being careful in your choice of terminology is imperative. Without being attuned to appropriate language, trusted relationships may be jeopardized based on a perception of prejudice.

Establishing Advisory Boards

Fusion centers will only gain the trust of the communities and agencies they serve if they are open and transparent in describing the purposes and goals of their activities. The nature of information gathering and collection raises concerns among many people in local communities, where there are widely held perceptions that information gathering, collection, and reporting about suspicious activity can be perceived as targeting immigrant and minority communities. Only by showing that fusion center operations are fully transparent, and providing an effective mechanism through which community concerns and perceptions can be addressed, will the community view the fusion center as an ally. Having an advisory board that includes representatives from local immigrant and minority communities can also greatly assist in addressing these perceptions.

Advisory boards provide policy guidance and can address issues of concern to fusion center customers as well as the surrounding community. In the drive for transparency, using an advisory board to review and discuss policy eliminates the sense that decisions are made in private, and can help dispel the perception that fusion center and law enforcement activities are routinely used to target immigrant and minority groups.

❖ **The role of the advisory board in representing the broader community.** Sometimes the fusion center is governed by a board that represents only certain agencies. Generally, these more limited boards are populated only by government or law enforcement officials, with few or no public members. Advisory board membership should be broadly based, with representatives from a cross-section of agencies who use or contribute to the fusion process.

❖ **Community involvement in an advisory board.** It may be useful to consider establishing a separate community advisory board as well as to have community members join the overall agency board. Having community members in this role allows fusion centers a leverage point to an even greater community audience and to deliver the message of transparency. Negative perceptions and fears can be better addressed when all relevant parties are a part of the discussion and have an opportunity to learn the facts and then raise any issues of concern. In addition, the community advisory board should be responsible for educating the community on the importance of building trusting relationships with law enforcement and the role of fusion centers. To ensure and maintain credibility, the advisory board should also establish a redress process for community concerns or complaints requiring resolution. There should then be a process in place to communicate this back to the agency advisory board.

❖ **Advisory boards must have input into the decision-making process.** Significant decisions and proposed policies should be brought before the advisory board, allowing members to discuss the issues involved and offer advice. For advisory boards to operate effectively, advice provided should be carefully considered, and reasons provided if advice is not accepted.

Providing Meaningful and Independent Audit and Oversight.

THERE ARE SIGNIFICANT CONCERNS WITHIN MANY COMMUNITIES REGARDING THE COLLECTION, STORAGE, SHARING, AND DISSEMINATION OF INFORMATION BY LAW ENFORCEMENT. Consequently, it is important that each fusion center also have a process in place to audit its data gathering, collection, usage, and storage to make sure that the center's privacy, civil rights, and civil liberties policies are being rigorously implemented. Failure to address these concerns will undermine the community's confidence in law enforcement. Here are some methods for instituting auditing processes:

❖ Use peer review and evaluation, where trained staff members from other fusion centers conduct regular audits of individual fusion centers. Using staff in this manner is beneficial for the employees involved in the audit, as it enhances their sensitivity to privacy, civil rights and civil liberties issues that must have a high priority. It also provides an audit team that is familiar with generally accepted information and intelligence practices, including the requirements of 28 CFR Part 23.

❖ Form an audit committee with broader representation, including well-respected members of the local community who have expertise in the issues involved and are eligible to access the data required for audit. Using a diverse team consisting of individuals who have knowledge of law enforcement policies and practices and the law, such as former state Attorneys General, District Attorneys, law school deans, or other respected public figures, provide added credibility to the audit process.

❖ Make audits public undertakings, with a summary of the results made public to ensure transparency. The standards applied should be noted in a report that identifies any gaps and a gap mitigation plan. Without transparency, public trust will not be developed, losing one important advantage of the audit process.

❖ Conduct audits on a regular, scheduled basis, at least once a year, reviewing a random sample of data files, intelligence reports, and related materials.

Establishing Knowledge about Fusion Centers

As with the SAR process, the fusion center needs to develop written documentation that explains to its various customers, to include local law enforcement, the mission of the center, how it operates, how it receives and disseminates information, and what officers can expect from an analysis of the information they provide. The documentation should include Q&A to help local law enforcement address any issues that might arise about fusion centers and their role in the community.

The fusion center should also make expansive use of Fusion Liaison Officers/ Terrorism Liaison Officers FLO/TLOs to get the message out to police agencies and others, as well as bring back to the fusion center issues of concern to those groups.

BEING USEFUL TO LOCAL POLICE. Local police agencies are, by their very purpose, major clients of fusion centers. Regularly surveying local law enforcement, and other customers, about their needs is important to ensuring that the fusion center is providing value. If local law enforcement feels that a fusion center is not contributing to operations, then they won't use its resources.

Some local police agencies, particularly in smaller communities, need research assistance in the conduct of major investigations. Many police agencies seek information that puts national events in a context that shows how the local policing and community environment may be impacted. Others want analysis across boundaries so they get a broader picture than is possible from only their internal data. Recognizing that each fusion center has a defined mission, if that mission doesn't encompass issues that local agencies feel are important, the fusion center may be viewed as nonresponsive and ineffective. For example, "clip and paste" bulletins without locally relevant analysis may be of little value, since most police personnel read the newspapers and watch television news daily. The challenge for fusion centers is to ensure that they are providing additional context for those operating in the local environment.

BEING USEFUL TO COMMUNITIES. Police are not the only beneficiaries of information sharing. Local communities stand to benefit as well. But local communities—particularly civil rights, civil liberties, immigrant and minority groups—often have different concerns about information sharing, fusion centers, and SAR than do local police. It is important to understand those perspectives and determine how best to address them through fusion center policies and processes.

❖ Always assume that products produced by the fusion center—even specialized products that may not be intended for the general public—will be read by impacted communities and will reach unintended audiences. Fusion centers should have a production process and policy in place prior to dissemination that includes a thorough review by management to ensure the paper is consistent with cultural norms, community issues, indications of bias, and constitutionally protected activities to avoid statements or analysis that violates these basic standards.

- Ensure that all products and reports go beyond just publicizing an event or situation by also providing a context that relates how that information might impact the local community. This includes framing the material in a manner that helps the community to understand the risk to the community if something bad happens (e.g., if a factory that handles hazardous materials gets hit with a bomb, what the consequences would be to the surrounding localities).

- Regularly survey local police and communities about the value they perceive in analytical products provided by the fusion center. Local agencies will only provide the most useful information if they receive value in return.

- Privacy, civil rights, and civil liberties concerns must have the highest priority in order to allay public concerns about how information is gathered, collected, and used.

- Privacy, civil rights, and civil liberties policies developed by fusion centers should receive community review prior to being adopted or significantly modified. There should be no secret about the development and modification of these policies. The more transparency with the public during the development and change process, the greater trust the community will have in the center's privacy, civil rights, and civil liberties protection policy. Completed privacy, civil rights, and civil liberties policies should be publicly posted to the fusion center's website.

- Fusion centers must recognize when information is received that reflects a constitutionally protected activity. There must be a mechanism to ensure that improper assumptions are not made from such activity and they do not serve as the basis for documenting suspicious behavior. Even with adequate training of analysts, there needs to be independent review of information gathering and analytical products to ensure that this does not occur.

- Wide distribution of the center's privacy policy should be undertaken, available on the web site of the fusion center, and distributed through local law enforcement agencies participating in fusion center activities.

RECOMMENDATIONS FOR LOCAL LAW ENFORCEMENT

Local police can build effective relationships of trust with the community while strengthening their commitment to information sharing and suspicious activity reporting if they are transparent about their intent and the processes by which they do their work, and honestly engage to address community members on issues of concern.

Establishing Officer Knowledge of the NSI Process

In alignment with the NSI training, law enforcement should develop an internal policy for SAR and other information, setting forth its purpose and processes as well as summarizing the privacy, civil rights, and civil liberties issues that members of the community have raised about the dangers of information gathering, collection, storage, sharing, and analysis. It is important that officers understand these community issues so they can respond intelligently if asked about them. The policy needs to be accompanied by training and orientation to the policy and clearly indicate the roles officers are expected to play. The importance of transparency in the information gathering, collection, and analysis process must be stressed, as well as the length law enforcement goes to protect privacy, civil rights and civil liberties. To participate in the NSI, fusion center sites must participate in three separate but coordinated training initiatives specifically created for law enforcement executives, analytic/investigative personnel, and line officers, which could be used at the local level for all law enforcement as well as for community leaders and advocates.

❖ Ensure that officers understand how a carefully implemented SAR capability can contribute to the safety of the community.

ESTABLISHING RELATIONSHIPS BETWEEN OFFICERS AND FUSION CENTERS.
Local law enforcement should reach out to their designated fusion center and establish a relationship and develop some common business processes for how they can work together as well as how they can work together with the communities they serve. By establishing and enhancing regular communication, law enforcement and fusion center personnel can reduce the possibility of erroneous or culturally insensitive information from being made public.

❖ Local, state, and tribal law enforcement need to work with the fusion center to ensure the availability of written documentation articulating the mission of the center: how it operates, how it receives and disseminates information, and what others can expect from an analysis of the information they provide. The documentation should include Q&A to help local law enforcement address any issues that might arise about fusion centers and their role in the community.

❖ More expansive use of FLO/TLO programs can assist in a better understanding of the purpose of the fusion center by police agencies and others as well as bring back to the fusion center issues of concern to those groups.

DEFINING AND DEVELOPING TRUSTING RELATIONSHIPS FOR OFFICERS.
The importance of police officers establishing trusting relationships with communities, particularly immigrant and minority communities, is critical if issues of crime and terrorism are to be addressed in a manner that builds the confidence and trust of that community. Trusting relationships must be established prior to a crisis so when a crisis occurs, the community will quickly come forth and offer assistance to the police agency. The experience of chiefs/sheriffs who have established such relationships have shown the strong impact those relationships can have when police actions inadvertently cause serious harm and the department is working to maintain community trust.

❖ Ensure that officers understand that honesty and openness are critical. Stress the importance of listening as a precursor to a basic relationship evolving into a relationship of trust. Communities want police officers to understand their perspectives, not necessarily to totally agree with them.

❖ Encourage officers to use these relationships to better understand how neighborhood residents view crime, disorder, and terrorism prevention. Such relationships also provide officers with an understanding of cultural norms in immigrant and minority communities, assisting officers to understand behaviors that are common and not suspicious. Understanding these perspectives also provides officers with information that can be used when other citizens complain about such normative behavior that they consider suspicious.

❖ Articulate to all officers the importance of developing and sustaining relationships with diverse segments of the community, encouraging officers to seek out and engage neighborhood leaders in discussions about issues of concern to them relative to community safety, crime control, and terrorism prevention.

❖ Continue regular outreach to community leaders to better understand their perception of policing issues, engaging them in sharing ideas for effective crime prevention strategies, even when there is no immediate crisis or particular crisis response objective.

❖ Reach out to communities prior to implementing new policies that impact community perception of the police or that address issues of concern to immigrant and minority residents to obtain community perspective on the new policy.

❖ Provide feedback to community members on the results of suggestions they have made about policing strategy or issues related to crime and terrorism prevention. Even if the suggestions will not be implemented, communicate that fact and the reasons why. Lack of follow-up is viewed by the community as a lack of interest and respect by the police.

❖ Provide guidance, training, and assistance to officers in developing relationships with immigrant and minority communities. Have officers practice initiating discussions with individuals and groups with whom they have had little contact in the past. Focus on the listening skills required and the need for followup with the community.

PROVIDE DIVERSITY THROUGHOUT THE FABRIC OF POLICING. Even the highest quality information collection, analysis and dissemination process can be undercut if immigrant and minority community members do not see diversity in the police workforce—not only among street officers but among staff assigned to the analytical function—they will have only limited confidence in the quality of work being undertaken. Just as diverse thought processes and perspectives can improve the intelligence process, officers of diverse backgrounds can improve effectiveness in the community.

❖ Issue a policy stating that diversity throughout the department is a high priority, reflecting the desire that the composition of the police agency reflect the community it serves. Aggressively act to make that policy a reality.

❖ Broaden outreach in the recruitment process to engage neighborhood leaders in identifying potential candidates. Develop position advertisements that reflect positively on the policing profession, as well as reflect an understanding of law enforcement issues of importance to local minority and immigrant communities.

❖ Make certain that internal police specialist assignments are open to people of diverse backgrounds. Qualified officers with diverse backgrounds should be considered for positions in every unit, particularly intelligence analysis and other specialties where diverse viewpoints and community relations are especially valuable.

❖ Confirm that there is a mentoring program within the department to support bright, capable personnel in advancing their careers, and ensure that mentor relationships advance diversity rather than hinder it.

ANSWERING COMMUNITY QUESTIONS. The community often only has a cursory understanding of policing procedures and how information sharing, analysis, and dissemination occur, and the laws that govern these procedures. Given the fears that immigrants may bring with them about law enforcement and their experiences in their home countries, they may have many questions about American law enforcement. Likewise, there are events in U.S. history reflecting serious tensions between police and various ethnic and minority communities, and immigrants will likely have questions about current policing processes, how abuses are avoided, and perceived grievances addressed.

The best mechanisms for addressing these concerns are transparency and a willingness to answer questions raised by residents and civil rights and civil liberties organizations in a factual and direct manner.

❖ Prepare answers to questions commonly asked by the community relating to policing and gathered from discussions with community leaders and civil rights and civil liberties advocates. Full disclosure and truthfulness is important. If the answer to a question is unknown when asked, tell the questioner that you will seek to find the answer and get back to them.

❖ When listening to residents or businesspeople describe their concerns about policing, fusion centers, or the SAR process, let them express their thoughts without becoming defensive, working to understand their perspective. Recognize that when community groups get their first opportunity to air concerns, they often include a variety of issues that may be beyond your control. Treating them with respect, listening carefully, and trying to understand their perspectives will go a long way toward developing a relationship of trust.

❖ Consider holding roundtables or focus groups to regularly obtain the sense of how the community views policing initiatives, such as SAR information and fusion centers. The roundtables held for the Building Communities of Trust initiative resulted in many concerns being put on the table in the communities that sponsored these discussions, with generally positive results once the discussions progressed.

❖ Recognize the importance of listening to the community in all types of situations. For example, when engaging in proactive neighborhood drug raids or other targeted policing actions, assign designated officers to answer resident's questions when they come out of their homes to observe the actions, rather than just telling people to "stand back as it is a police matter."

ADDRESSING COMMUNITY CONCERNS. Communities have numerous concerns regarding information sharing and almost any activity involving what is commonly termed "intelligence." These concerns reflect fears that constitutionally protected activities will be monitored and documented by the police; that personal information will be collected when there has been no violation of the law; and that there is only limited oversight of these processes that can have a negative impact on freedoms guaranteed by the U.S. and State Constitutions. Ignoring these concerns can lead to the perception that nefarious activity is occurring within fusion centers and as a part of the suspicious activity reporting. Police must be aware that there is also a substantial fear among community members about being typecast as having "ratted out" others in the community if information is shared with law enforcement, even about law breakers.

❖ Ensure that the department has a strong privacy, civil rights, and civil liberties protection policy in place and trains to that policy. Use an audit process—described above—to ensure that all activity falls within that policy.

❖ Engage with the civil rights and civil liberties community in developing and addressing the policy so as to gain insight into the issues of concern, and see that those issues are addressed in the policy and its audit process.

❖ Make the privacy, civil rights, and civil liberties protection policy public and widely available to any interested party, as well as posted on public websites.

❖ Understand the dynamics of racial profiling and how bias can impact officer (and analyst) decision-making. Provide checks on products to ensure that bias is not unintentionally reflected.

❖ Establish policy and training to ensure that officers do not inappropriately use race, religion, and other individual other constitutionally protected characteristics unrelated to the worth of the individual as characteristics indicative of suspicious behavior. Provide training materials that show situations in which bias has been inappropriately used in decision-making, and how to deal with comparable situations in an unbiased manner.

- ❖ Include situational items on intentional and unintentional bias in promotional examinations to measure whether candidates understand the difference and know proper responses when such use occurs.

- ❖ Develop training for police officers that captures their imagination and empowers them to make full use of the new information capabilities that the fusion center and the NSI provide.

- ❖ Create training about bias and its impact on the information sharing environment that assists officers to understand how bias is destructive to important policing objectives.

- ❖ Work with the local community to address community fears about being perceived as informants when sharing information about those who are or who may be breaking the law. This includes verifying that confidentiality is tightly protected and increasing understanding that preventing crime benefits the safety of the entire community.

MOVING BEYOND COMMUNITY RELATIONS. Developing trusting relationships with the community is more than simply assigning officers to engage in police-community relations; it involves spending time with the community discussing issues of concern, collaborating and responding to issues of crime and public safety, and interacting respectfully with community members, regardless of their views and concerns. Police officials need to:

- ❖ Ensure that officers are trained to distinguish between behaviors associated with terrorism-related and general crime and those behaviors that are legal, cultural and/or constitutionally protected.

- ❖ Make sure that every officer on field duty knows how to approach persons from diverse backgrounds and engage in positive, meaningful conversation relating to the neighborhood.

- ❖ Require that officers assigned to neighborhood policing must maintain a strong ongoing dialog with neighborhood residents and business people.

- ❖ Train walking officers to provide a "felt" presence throughout the neighborhood; if walking in pairs, make contact with each passerby (even if only by a nod) and don't converse only with your partner.

❖ Encourage field officers to understand the community's sense of important issues relating to life in the neighborhood and concerns about crime and disorder.

❖ Provide officers training on communication skills as each officer's comfort level and experience may vary when it comes to working with the community.

SUMMARY

Relationships of trust will not be established until key community leaders understand the intent of the information sharing environment and the preventive role that fusion centers and the SAR process plays in protecting the community from crime and violence. A fully transparent explanation can be the foundation for broad community understanding of the importance of these initiatives as well as the critical privacy, civil rights, and civil liberties protections that are in place.

Understanding the Importance of Information Sharing

Using the all-crimes approach, the police agency should present information sharing as a "community positive" concept, focused on identifying those who prey on others in the community through criminal acts. In describing these concepts, the police agency should stress the overall objective of preventing crime and terrorist acts and the importance of all community institutions working to prevent young people from being drawn into criminal actions that will negatively impact their future.

❖ Engage community leadership in both private and open forums, where concepts are discussed and questions answered. Public forums should also be held, such as the Building Communities of Trust roundtables, encouraging diverse community groups to raise any concerns related to government identification and tracking of criminal activity.

❖ Provide community leadership with regular reports on fusion center and SAR activities. Simply advising the community on what fusion centers do and how the NSI operates will be insufficient to gain the support of the impacted community. Regular reporting to community leadership is important, and also contributes to building long-term sustainable trusting relationships.

Bring the Community into the Problem-Solving Process

Have representatives of the community participate in orienting new police officers to minority and immigrant communities as a part of the recruit training process, with the training occurring in the community, not at the academy. This provides the community with a stake in the success of new officers and provides the officers with the contacts upon which relationships of trust can be built.

❖ Form police advisory councils—both department-wide and in decentralized commands, including members from immigrant and minority communities. Each neighborhood police commander should have an advisory council that meets regularly, where open discussion occurs about crime prevention and control strategies and questions and concerns about police policy and strategy can be addressed.

❖ Policing challenges related to crime and community safety should be brought before these advisory councils, seeking input and guidance in solving ongoing problems that impact crime, disorder, and potential terrorist acts. Solutions should include actions to be taken not only by the police but by the community as well.

❖ Develop a community-centric brochure describing the fusion center, the all crimes approach, data protections, and how the center operates to protect each member of the community.

Understand and Use Appropriate Language and Terminology before Taking Action

To avoid misusing terms such as radical, radicalism, extremist, and violent extremism, the police, fusion center personnel, and analysts must understand the culture of communities that are impacted by their various investigative approaches.

❖ Police officers, crime analysts, and intelligence analysts cannot use race, ethnicity, national origin, or religious affiliation as factors to support suspicion and trigger investigations. There is an inherent danger in publicly highlighting the views espoused by violent extremists in such a way that those views are perceived to be held by the majority of an immigrant or minority community. To do so can be counterproductive for law enforcement and could inhibit the development of trust between law enforcement and the community, since it is likely that these communities could find themselves typecast in a prejudicial way , blaming law enforcement and, more generally, the government, for societal discrimination.

APPENDIXES

Appendix A: Terminology

LOCAL LAW ENFORCEMENT. This includes public sector law enforcement agencies at the state, local, tribal, and territorial level. Private security is considered a separate category of law enforcement.

COLLABORATION. Collaboration means equal sharing in the development of strategies, tactics, and programs. Those who are at the table as collaborators all have an equal say in the problem-solving process. When a collaborative effort is undertaken by a governmental agency with members of a constituent group, those who are invited to join in the effort have a responsibility to understand each person's perspective and respect those positions. Collaboration is more than listening; it is also consultation. It means working together by creating an environment of mutual respect in order to identify an outcome or solution that best addresses a given issue.

Effective collaboration is not only joint decision-making about how efforts will be undertaken. Collaborating with the community, for example, goes beyond deciding on a course of action and informing the community of that decision. The community must be brought into discussions before a solution or program is designed in order to have the necessary understanding of how the solution or program was conceived, what it really seeks to accomplish, and how the community shares responsibility for the outcomes.

TRANSPARENCY. Transparency is a key ingredient in establishing trust with local communities and means that the processes and policies used by government in handling information must be fully evident and understandable.

DIVERSITY. This is the inclusion of persons from different races, religions, gender, and cultures in organizations, programs, initiatives, or collaborative efforts. In policing and special initiatives such as fusion centers, diversity is critical if the population being served is to have trust and confidence in the outcomes of these activities. There are many ways of displaying diversity and setting a tone of inclusion within a fusion center or police force to visibly demonstrate an active commitment to involve and learn from people who may understand the broad range of perspectives within the community.

Many executives acknowledge the importance of diversity, and ensuring a diverse work force is critical to the success of activities that must embrace the community. In particular, necessary diversity in the analytic workforce requires broad outreach to identify the right mix of individuals with the necessary skills, competencies and attributes to be successful at analytical work—while at the same time incorporating an understanding of the community's diverse culture into the process.

VIOLENT EXTREMISM. While extremism may be considered the advocacy of extreme political measures to achieve desired ends, such behavior becomes a concern when violence becomes a tactic to achieve those ends. It is important to differentiate extremism from violent extremism. Extremists have specific, sometimes uncompromising views, which may be communicated in numerous ways that are protected by the Constitution. As a result, law enforcement cannot and should not consider an extremist view as potentially violent. For a person or group to be considered violent extremists, they must specifically advocate for or engage in violent activities.

GUIDANCE. Recommendations to assist in the development of trusting relationships with local communities. This includes strategies and actions to accomplish common objectives, based upon analysis of best practices.

MINORITY COMMUNITIES. Minority communities in this discussion are those communities that have special identify as a particular culture or which make up less than a majority part of the political environment. As such, minority communities (of which immigrant communities are often a part) may feel estranged from the larger society and perceive that others do not understand their culture and are insensitive to their concerns and issues. Even communities that make up a large part of a city may be considered "minority communities" because they do not have access to the decision-making process that determines how government operates or the economic power to influence the community politic.

PARTNERSHIP. An effective partnership is a collaborative relationship focused on a common goal. Communities can partner with police to develop safe neighborhoods; schools can partner with parents to provide quality education; and community organizations can partner with police and other units of government to undertake activities that benefit the community. In this sense, partnership means accepting shared responsibility for the strategy developed and the quality of implementation.

Police and other public safety officials often ask communities for their reactions to new policies, but usually after the policies are developed. Rarely do local agencies first partner with the community in developing or implementing a policy or new initiative. While maintaining that type of partnership is a complex and demanding task, and sustaining momentum a common challenge, establishing robust partnerships between stakeholders working on mutual goals is a positive step.

IDENTITY PROFILING. Identity profiling is most commonly understood as the discriminatory practice of targeting individuals for suspicion based solely on the individual's race, ethnicity, religion, or national origin. The term came into use after it was alleged that the New Jersey State Police targeted Blacks and Latinos for traffic stops on the New Jersey Turnpike after the police had received (incorrect) information that drug trafficking on the turnpike was carried out predominately by those groups.

Questions naturally arise when citizens are perceived to be inappropriately singled out for law enforcement purposes, e.g., traffic stops, airport screening, etc. As a result, if the community sees that law enforcement or others do not treat members of all groups with respect and listen without judgment, there is an assumption that such treatment results from profiling—even when identity has little to do with the interaction. It is important that law enforcement and other public safety officials listen to what people have to say and not take action based on preconceived notions.

RADICALIZATION. Although incorrectly defined by some as "violent extremism that targets society through violent acts," the official definition in Webster's Dictionary of the term "radical" is "tending or disposed to make extreme changes in existing views, habits, institutions or conditions." Radicals are those individuals who believe and espouse nonmainstream sociopolitical viewpoints. There is nothing illegal about being radical in one's beliefs—expressing one's beliefs and opinions is a constitutionally protected freedom. However, it is illegal to carry out a criminal act in furtherance of those beliefs and that is the difference between violent extremism and radicalization or general extremism. The line between radicalism and violent extremism can be difficult to see when espoused beliefs run contrary to the majority public opinion. But in a democracy, where freedom of speech and peaceful assembly are core constitutional values, political viewpoints by themselves do not cause the violent destruction of society.

Appendix B: Background

The Development of Fusion Centers

There are 72 recognized state and major urban area fusion centers that are owned and operated by the states or jurisdiction in which they are located. The common goal in creating these information fusion centers is to identify risks to community safety through criminal and homeland security related information sharing and collaboration. To that end, these fusion centers provide stakeholders with a focal point for the receipt, analysis, and dissemination of all-threat and all-crimes information. In operating as an adjunct to the 750,000 law enforcement officers across the nation, the centers serve as a primary focal point for the Federal Government to work with state, local, tribal, and territorial entities to protect the nation from terrorism and other threats or hazards.

Some of the first centers to be established focused primarily on providing investigative case support to local law enforcement. Those activities were welcomed by local agencies that didn't have the resources to undertake such activities themselves. Other centers reviewed information from national information networks, including news media and other law enforcement agencies, repackaging the information to address local concerns. At the early stages of fusion center development, there were no common national standards for their organization or operation.

In time, federal, state, and local governments recognized the importance of developing and maintaining common standards to ensure that fusion centers met basic levels of data protection and adequately addressed privacy, civil rights, and civil liberties protections, security policies, and related issues. In order to instill greater consistency, federal, state and local officials identified a set of baseline capabilities that are critical to ensuring standardized operations. The Baseline Capabilities for State and Major Urban Area Fusion Centers, released in September 2008 by the US Department of Justice (DOJ), Department of Homeland Security (DHS), and the Global Justice Information Sharing Initiative, identifies 12 core capabilities and provides specific instructions on how to achieve each capability. Today, with the incorporation of a standardized nationwide suspicious activity reporting process as part of the information flow to fusion centers, common privacy, civil rights, and civil liberties standards that apply to fusion centers are being strengthened even further.

Fusion centers are uniquely positioned to bring significant value to the information sharing environment by including analysis on what information might mean for the local jurisdiction and in assessing potential risk to the community. Fusion centers have come to recognize that they must demonstrate a return on investment if they are to be viewed by local law enforcement and homeland security partners as adding value. In the context of BCOT, efforts are underway to provide civil liberties and civil rights training to fusion center analysts in order to ensure that reporting does not make inappropriate assumptions about culture, race, ethnicity, radicalism or extremism, and other constitutionally protected activities.

The Nationwide Suspicious Activity Reporting (SAR) Initiative (NSI)

The NSI provides a capacity for gathering, documenting, processing, analyzing, and sharing SARs reasonably indicative of activity that may be related to terrorism, while also ensuring that privacy, civil rights, and civil liberties are adequately protected in accordance with federal, state, and local laws and regulations. Much of general SAR reporting may relate to potential criminal action, from drug dealing to equipment purchases that are clearly suspicious. But through careful vetting and analysis (both at the reporting level, and later at the fusion center if the information meets the standard for sharing ISE information), linking accurate observations from various sources can prevent crime.

In many instances, suspicious activity relating to crime and terrorism is observed by members of communities in which that activity occurs. Members of the community who see that activity will only be willing to report it if they trust the police and they feel that the police have legitimacy in their community. Absent that trust, police will have little knowledge of activities that, if properly addressed, can protect the community from further harm.

The NSI process provides a mechanism for collecting such information in a manner that protects the source, is carefully evaluated to ensure the safeguarding of constitutionally protected activity, and links that which is actually suspicious with other observations that may indicate criminal activity. Through this process, controls over information collection, sharing, analysis, and reporting are carefully reviewed to meet important privacy, civil rights, and civil liberties standards, and designed to include full transparency of process, adherence to standards, and the implementation of audit and redress capabilities.

In the development of community policing, it has long been assumed that to be effective every officer must have trusted relationships. While that is a meaningful goal, lessons learned have shown that specially trained officers who focus full time in facilitating communication between leadership of those communities and the police executive can be very beneficial. Fusion centers can leverage the relationships that local police have established with their communities. Forging a cooperative relationship with local law enforcement, particularly in communities that have substantial minority or immigrant populations, will ensure that the fusion center better understands the community they are designed to support. At the same time, fusion centers can provide areawide analysis of general crime and related issues that provide local police with a perspective on the broader issues in their region, and assist in identifying significant patterns and trends. In this way, both fusion centers and local police can benefit together from strong collaborative relationships.

Appendix C: How to Get Started

This document details the specific steps and process for putting together a successful Building Communities of Trust (BCOT) Roundtable event.

Pre-Event Planning:

❖ Assemble a local planning team with representatives from the local community, law enforcement, and fusion center. This group should have the preliminary meeting at least 10 weeks before the anticipated date, and should meet on a regular basis up to the event.

❖ Select a date and time for the event.

   ❈ When choosing this date, take into consideration federal, state, and religious holidays and observances, as well as other cultural and religious sensitivities (e.g., Fridays are recognized a Muslim day of prayer).

   ❈ In the pilot program, roundtable events averaged 4 hours, so the time of day needs to be taken into account too to ensure diverse representation.

❖ Create an invitation list of law enforcement, fusion center personnel, community representatives, and advocates.

   ❈ Limiting the number of attendees to 35–40 provides the best opportunity for dialog and productive discussion.

   ❈ Law enforcement should only represent 25 percent or less of those attending the roundtable.

   ❈ To ensure transparency, planning teams are strongly encouraged to engage local advocacy groups (e.g., ACLU, Anti-Defamation League, etc.).

❖ Identify a venue.

   ❈ If possible, use a neutral site such as a community center or local college/university.

   ❈ Try to choose a central location that is easily accessible (e.g., public transportation, parking).

❖ Should you decide to provide refreshments during the meeting, take into account dietary restrictions, particularly with regard to religious beliefs.

❖ Invitations and any included read-ahead materials should be sent out 4 weeks prior to the roundtable—follow-up phone calls may be necessary to ensure diverse participation.

❖ Select a facilitator who will engage all participants and keep the dialog on subject.

❖ Set an agenda, identifying all presenters and topics to be discussed.

❖ For the room layout, a U shape setting provides everyone the opportunity to see one another and is most productive for conversation. It is also helpful to have tabletop microphones for attendees and a portable microphone for the facilitator.

❖ A week before the event, have one final meeting of the planning team, to include all presenters.

❖ Have all materials printed, including tabletop name tents and/or name tags.

Day of the Roundtable Event:

❖ The planning team should arrive early to check on the setup of the room and handle any other last-minute details.

   ❖ If name tents are created for the event, strategically place them on the table so law enforcement and community/advocacy representatives are equally distributed around the table .

   ❖ Set up a registration area. Be sure to have extra materials and name tags/tents on hand for any people who may attend who were not on the RSVP list.

   ❖ Capture any missing contact information at this time so attendees can be included in future meetings/events.

❖ Have a designated person record meeting notes/minutes, which should be distributed to all attendees after the meeting. Be sure to announce that someone will be recording, so if representatives would like a statement to be off the record, they are aware of this option.

After the Event:

❖ Finalize meeting notes and distribute to all attendees.

❖ Follow up with any materials or requests for information.

Appendix D: Advisory Committee

Building Communities of Trust Initiative
Advisory Committee Participants
Washington, District of Columbia, May 11, 2009

Ms. Christina Abernathy
Institute for Intergovernmental
Research

Mr. John Amaya
Mexican American Legal Defense
and Education Fund

Ms. Katherine Black
Office of the Program Manager,
Information Sharing Environment

Director Michael T. Bosacker
Minnesota Bureau of Criminal
Apprehension

Ms. Mary Ellen Callahan
U.S. Department of Homeland
Security

Mr. John Cohen
Office of the Program Manager,
Information Sharing Environment

Ms. Susan Courtwright-Rodriguez
U.S. Department of Homeland
Security

Mr. Robert Cummings
Institute for Intergovernmental
Research

Mr. Mohamed Elibiary
Freedom and Justice Foundation

Ms. J. Elizabeth Farrell
Office of the Program Manager,
Information Sharing Environment

Mr. Michael German
American Civil Liberties Union

Mr. David D. Gersten
U.S. Department of Homeland
Security

Ms. Safiya Ghori-Ahmad
Muslim Public Affairs Council

Mr. Ken Hunt
U.S. Department of Homeland
Security

Director Vernon Keenan
Georgia Bureau of Investigation

Dr. George Kelling
Rutgers University

Ms. Eva Kleederman
Office of the Director of National
Intelligence

Lieutenant Ron Leavell
Washington State Fusion Center

Ms. Hillary Lerner
U.S. Department of Homeland
Security

Ms. Nancy C. Libin
U.S. Department of Justice

Mr. Ritchie A. Martinez
Arizona Department of Public Safety

Commander Joan T. McNamara
Los Angeles Police Department

Ms. Kristen Moncada
U.S. Department of Justice

Ms. Miriam Moore
U.S. Department of Homeland
Security

Mr. Thomas J. O'Reilly
U.S. Department of Justice

Ms. Terri Pate
Institute for Intergovernmental
Research

Director Russell M. Porter
Iowa Department of Public Safety

Ms. Jenny Presswalla
U.S. Department of Homeland
Security

Ms. Diane Ragans
Institute for Intergovernmental
Research

**Assistant Director Ronald C.
Ruecker**
Federal Bureau of Investigation

Mr. Irfan Saeed
U.S. Department of Homeland
Security

Ms. Amy Schapiro
U.S. Department of Justice

Mr. Kerry Sleeper
Office of the Program Manager,
Information Sharing Environment

Reverend DeForest "Buster" Soaries
First Baptist Church of Lincoln
Gardens

Mr. Robert L. Stewart
Bobcat Training and Consulting, Inc.

Mr. Haris Tarin
Muslim Public Affairs Council

Mr. Robert Wasserman
Strategic Policy Partnership

Josh K. Weerasinghe, Ph.D.
Office of the Program Manager,
Information Sharing Environment

Mr. John J. Wilson
Institute for Intergovernmental
Research